Cornerstones of Freedom

The Story of
THE
ERIE CANAL

by R. Conrad Stein

Illustrated by Keith Neely

CHILDRENS PRESS ™

CHICAGO

Library of Congress Cataloging in Publication Data

Stein, R. Conrad.
  The story of the Erie Canal.

  (Cornerstones of freedom)
  Includes index.
  Summary: An account of the early nineteenth-century
construction of the 363-mile canal connecting Albany
and Buffalo.
  1. Erie Canal (N.Y.)—History—Juvenile literature.
[1. Erie Canal (N.Y.)—History] I. Neely, Keith,
1943-   ill. II. Title. III. Series.
HE396.E6S74 1985   386'.48'09747   84-28525
ISBN 0-516-04682-9   AACR2

In the eastern United States, the Appalachian Mountains rise into the sky, lofty and majestic. But some two hundred years ago, it was nearly impossible for Americans to cross them. The mountain chain, which today is a scenic delight, was once a frustrating barrier to America's westward expansion.

Certainly a few pioneer farm families managed to cross the Appalachians by hiking over Indian trails while carrying their household goods on pack animals. Once they crossed the mountains, however, the settlers were entirely cut off from their countrymen in the East. In fact, their isolation was so complete that some politicians feared that a separate nation would develop west of the Appalachians.

In the early 1800s, large cities and a factory system grew in the East. Merchants hoped that a healthy trade would develop between western farmers and eastern city dwellers. The farmers could provide food for the cities while the factories produced manufactured goods for the farms. But blocking this perfect marriage between East and West was the ever-present Appalachian mountain chain that ran like a jagged wall from Canada to Alabama.

A few visionaries dreamed of building a ship canal that would cut through the mountains. However, most Americans believed that it would be impossible for their young country to construct such a canal. A waterway connecting the East with the West would have to stretch more than three hundred miles through untamed forests and over the mighty mountains. How would it be possible to dig such a canal? Who would pay for the construction? Even the brilliant Thomas Jefferson, whose ideas were usually a generation ahead of his time, said about the proposed canal: "It is a splendid project and may be executed a century hence. . . .But it is little short of madness to think of it at this day!"

Still, many Americans clung to the belief that it was possible to dig a canal through the western

wilderness. One of them was a remarkable New York named De Witt Clinton.

Clinton was tall and ruggedly handsome. Born into a wealthy family, he served terms as mayor of New York City and as governor of New York State. Whatever his job, Clinton threw himself into his work. As mayor, he galloped on horseback ahead of fire wagons so he could help the firemen string hoses. Many of his countrymen, including Thomas Jefferson, believed that De Witt Clinton would be a perfect candidate for the presidency. And he might have pursued the office had he not decided to channel his amazing energy into an enormous project. Early in the 1800s, De Witt Clinton became obsessed with the idea of building a westward canal through the wilderness of upper New York State.

Before the first shovel of earth could be turned, however, Clinton had to produce a staggering amount of money. The federal government thought the project was harebrained, and refused to allocate a penny toward it. So Clinton bullied and cajoled the legislators of New York State. Miraculously, he persuaded them to vote six million dollars to begin construction. Clinton assured the politicians that the state would regain the money through tolls charged on the canal. Nevertheless, six million dollars was an outrageous sum for the state to spend. At the time, only 1.3 million people lived in New York. The expenditure amounted to five dollars for every man, woman, and child in the state. In the early 1800s, five dollars was a lot of money and taxpayers were frugal.

On the bright morning of July 4, 1817, dignitaries gathered at Rome, New York to break ground for the new canal. Rome was in the middle of the proposed route. The planners started work there because they believed that the surrounding ground would prove easier to dig than other sections. It was no accident that the ceremonies took place on July 4—the most hallowed holiday celebrated by the young nation. De Witt Clinton had a fine sense of history. Besides, he needed publicity to persuade New Yorkers to spend even more tax money in the future. Brass bands played, fireworks crackled, and politicians made speeches. The last speaker said, "Let us proceed with the work."

Construction of the Erie Canal had officially
begun.

To the planners, the job ahead seemed as awesome
as moving mountains. From the Hudson River to
Lake Erie the great ditch would stretch 363 miles. It
would have to cross forests, span rivers, and cut
through hills. And, somehow, it would have to climb
the Appalachian Mountains.

On the construction site, trees tumbled and earth
turned. The proposed ditch was to be forty feet wide
at the surface, then slope downward to a width of
twenty-eight feet at the bottom. The waterway
would be only four feet deep. Next to the huge

ERIE CANAL

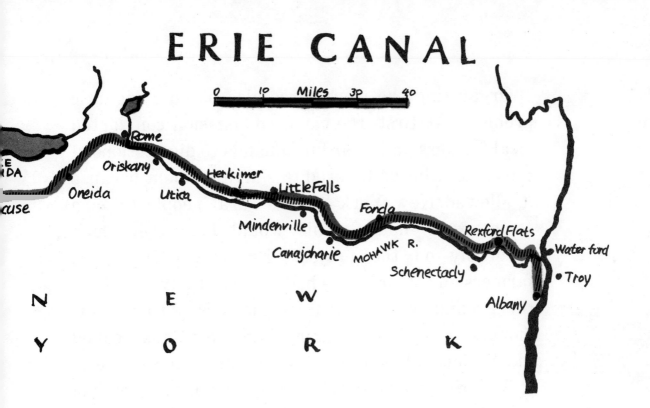

0 10 Miles 30 40

Rome
Oriskany
Oneida
Utica
Herkimer
Little Falls
Mindenville
Canajoharie
Fonda
MOHAWK R.
Rexford Flats
Waterford
Schenectady
Troy
Albany

N E W Y O R K

trench, workers cleared a towpath along which horses and mules would pull the canal boats.

From the beginning, the digging was beset by problems. Canal construction was a new activity in the United States. The canal commission that had been appointed to supervise construction had only a few engineers who had worked on canals before. In fact, the commission's two chief engineers were lawyers whose only background in engineering was a bit of land surveying. Plans for the project were so confused and incomplete that no one knew exactly where on Lake Erie the great ditch would end.

11

Organizing the work force also posed a gigantic problem. At first, the canal commission contracted local farmers and their hired hands to dig sections of the canal. Clinton favored this arrangement because it allowed New York State's rural people to earn some extra money. This would help them look favorably on the project. Frequently, however, farmers and their hands had to leave their shovels in the ground to tend to farm matters. After a few months, one observer claimed that the canal looked like "a dotted line of poorly dug, unfinished ditches."

A more practical solution to the labor problem came from abroad. For generations, farmers and workers had sailed away from impoverished Ireland bound for America's shores. By the early 1800s, approximately ten thousand Irish men and women were arriving each year to try their luck in the New World. When Irish newcomers learned that they could make money in the forests of upper New York State, they flocked to the project. Soon the canal was being built largely by Irish muscle.

Canal workers often spent grueling fourteen-hour days at their labor. They slept in work camps and rose to the call, "All out! Mush in the kettle!" This was only a "Soup's on!" type of expression, however.

The workers ate a good deal more than the hot cereal that was generally called mush. A typical breakfast included bacon, eggs, potatoes, and cornbread.

Work on the canal was backbreaking and continued even under the broiling sun or in torrential rains. At night, the exhausted men slept on hard wooden beds and had to fend off swarms of mosquitoes. The common laborer received a wage of eighty cents a day. This was good pay by an American worker's standards, but to the Irish

immigrant it was a fortune. Eighty cents a week was the average wage in Ireland.

Still, the Irish laborers had to work hard as well as adjust to the strangeness of an unfamiliar country. One canal historian said, "The country at the end of the voyage was rougher than anything the men had known in Ireland. Owls and wildcats in the woods kept them awake and scared at night. The first time a snake came into camp, the whole lot nearly deserted. There are no snakes in Ireland. They thought this one was the devil."

But even in their weariest moments, the Irish workers were a singing people. One unknown balladeer wrote this song about the magnitude of digging the Erie Canal:

When I came to this wonderful empire,
It filled me with the greatest surprise
To see such a great undertaking,
On the like I ne'er opened my eyes.

To see a full thousand brave fellows
At work among mountains so tall
To dig through the valleys so level,
Through rocks for to cut a canal.

The digging was speeded up by American inventive genius. At first, crews cut down trees along the route, but left the earth enmeshed with tough tree roots. The task of chopping through the roots was slow and arduous. Then some genius, whose name has been forgotten by history, designed a marvelous stump-pulling device. It was a huge two-wheeled, one-axle contraption that was positioned over a stump. With the aid of a chain and a pulley, the machine yanked the stubborn stump out of the earth, roots and all. Another invention created during the canal's construction pulled entire trees out of the ground.

STUMP PULLER

ROPE PULLED
BY HORSES

As the work progressed, engineers and workers overcame their lack of experience by dogged determination and trial and error. Each new mile of completed canal became a valuable lesson. Initially, seepage of water into a freshly dug ditch threatened to be a major problem. Then the men discovered that they could seal the canal's walls with a special clay found in New York's soil. With even more experience, the engineers learned how to prepare a unique cement that hardened even under water.

During the second year of construction, however, the men encountered an obstacle no one was prepared to meet. The canal route cut through a marshland known as Montezuma's Swamp. Local Cayuga

Indians warned the workers not to enter the swamp, but no one took the Indians' advice seriously. Then, when they started digging in the swamp, the workers were attacked by thick clouds of angry mosquitoes. According to one source, the mosquitoes "fell upon the diggers in hordes. The men came in with eyes swollen almost shut and hands so poisoned they could hardly wield their tools." It was not known then that certain mosquitoes carried the dreaded disease malaria. At least a thousand men working near the swamp fell ill, and many of them died. Chilly autumn weather finally put an end to the mosquitoes, and the workers dug their way out of the miserable Montezuma's Swamp.

Overseeing much of the work was the tireless De Witt Clinton. Early in the construction years, he served as governor of New York State, but he continually found excuses to leave his office and check on the canal's progress. At the work site, he paced up and down the long trench, wanting to see every fresh inch of digging. The official name of the project was the Grand Western Canal. History would call it the Erie Canal. But while it was being built, it was popularly called "Clinton's Ditch."

The first section of the canal opened in 1819, only two years after the ground breaking. The new waterway ran just fifteen miles, between Rome and Utica, New York. Infinitely more sweat, muscle, and pain lay ahead. Engineers and workers still had to face their most difficult challenge—the rugged Appalachian Mountains.

To cross the Appalachians and the other mountains along the route, the canal commission decided to build a lock canal. Locks are water-filled chambers with huge doors on either end. They are usually built in series up the face of a hill or a mountain. By closing the doors and pumping water into the chamber, a boat can be lifted, lock by lock, over a mountain and down the other side. Eighty-four locks, each ninety feet long and fifteen feet wide, were needed on the Erie Canal. The locks posed an engineering problem even more complicated than the digging.

The canal commission's engineers and workers learned how to build locks by the same painful methods they had learned how to dig the great ditch. They had no books or experienced men to consult. So they simply attacked the job and learned from their mistakes. Often the canal builders defied the few experts who did exist. At Little Falls, New York, the canal commission asked a consulting engineer how long it would take to build a particularly difficult set of locks. The engineer made a careful study and said, "three years." The canal commission then turned its crack crews to work and the men finished the project in three months.

The commission's supreme engineering triumph took place at a jagged mountain some twenty miles from Buffalo. There the canal had to rise sixty-six feet up a cliff of solid rock. Using explosives, workers blasted five sets of double locks out of the face of the cliff. They then created a perfectly functional and strangely beautiful set of watery stepping-stones for canal boats. The town that later

grew up around this set of locks was called, appropriately, Lockport.

Probably it was the construction at Lockport that inspired this verse of a popular song sung by canal workers:

> We are cutting the Ditch through the rocks,
> Through the rocks across the state, by heck!
> We are cutting the Ditch through the rocks,
> And we'll finish her off with stone locks,
> From the rocks across the state, by heck!
> From the rocks across the state.

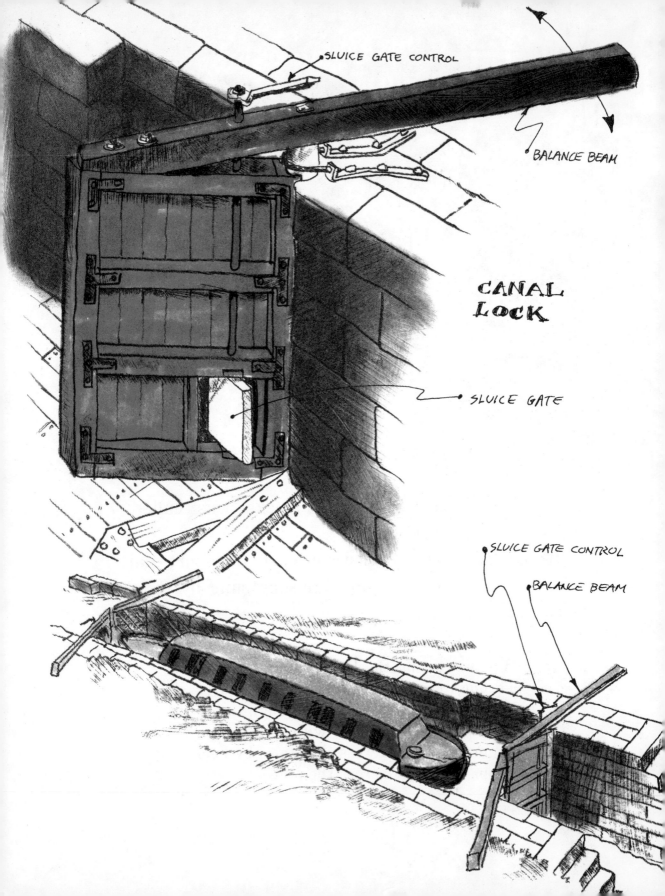

SLUICE GATE CONTROL

BALANCE BEAM

CANAL
LOCK

SLUICE GATE

SLUICE GATE CONTROL

BALANCE BEAM

In addition to locks, bridges had to be built so the canal could cross over natural rivers and streams. Eighteen bridges or aqueducts were built along the canal's route. With their graceful arches and sturdy construction, the aqueducts were the engineering marvels of their time. The largest aqueduct was at Crescent, about twelve miles from Albany. There, a bridge nearly two thousand feet long carried the canal over the Mohawk River.

Locks and aqueducts were the most spectacular structures built on the Erie Canal, but hundreds of less noticeable projects also went into the construction. An elaborate system of gates and sluices had to be created to supply water for the canal and to operate the locks. Emergency drains were dug to discharge water in case of heavy rain or a flood. Finally, a vast network of branch canals was created to allow local farmers access to the main canal.

While work progressed in the field, the canal project attracted enemies in New York's capital. The construction costs were skyrocketing. Its critics claimed that never in an eternity could revenue from the canal pay off its enormous debts. De Witt Clinton fought a continual political battle with the canal's foes. In 1822, the anti-canal politicians were so powerful that Clinton was defeated in his efforts to be renominated as governor of New York. But Clinton retained his membership in the canal commission. From that office, he fought to complete the project.

Aiding Clinton's plea was the revenue that began to flow in from finished sections of the canal. Opening the canal in sections was part of the overall grand plan. After the first small section was completed in 1819, another section almost eighty miles long was opened for traffic in 1820. By 1823, the canal extended as far as the Hudson River, its eastern boundary. Boat owners operated in these segments, and the tolls they paid brought in a substantial amount of money. Clinton used this toll revenue as an argument to convince New York taxpayers to carry the project to its conclusion.

Finally, in 1825, diggers reached Buffalo, on the

shores of Lake Erie. Although a thousand small chores remained, the great ditch was finished. It was an engineering masterpiece, and would prove to be the major highway of a new American empire.

On October 26, 1825, a parade led by a booming band marched down the main street of Buffalo, New York. At its head strode De Witt Clinton, again governor of New York. His pet project had taken almost ten years to complete. But today he walked proudly, befitting a man who had lived to see his impossible dream come true.

Clinton and other dignitaries boarded a canal boat
called the *Seneca Chief.* It was slated to be the first
boat to travel the entire length of the Erie Canal. As
the *Seneca Chief* pulled away from its moorings, men
on the outskirts of Buffalo fired a cannon. Another
cannon several miles east fired when its crew heard
the first blast. This triggered a row of cannons, all
stationed within earshot of each other, and stretch-
ing hundreds of miles across the woodlands of New
York State. The thundering chain reaction brought
the message to New York City that the great Erie
Canal was now open for business. The colorful open-

ing ceremony was called "the Wedding of the Waters."

From its beginning, the Erie Canal made money for the state of New York. In 1826, its first full year of operation, tolls paid by boat owners brought in more than three quarters of a million dollars. In nine years, revenue from the canal completely paid off its construction debts. The waterway continued to turn a profit until 1882, when tolls were finally abolished. By that time, the canal had paid for itself more than thirty times over.

The canal also fulfilled the original dreams of the planners. It connected the farms west of the Appalachians to the cities in the East. Before the canal opened, farm products from the West had to be carried by horses over crude mountain roads to the eastern cities. It cost western farmers a hundred dollars a ton to transport their sacks of flour to New York City. After the canal opened, that cost dropped to ten dollars a ton.

Eastern farm families flocked to the sprawling West via the new waterway. The canal passage spared them the arduous mountain crossing that earlier pioneers had had to endure. Settlers began to pour into the once-deserted woodlands of what are now the states of Ohio, Indiana, Illinois, and Michigan.

It took seven to ten days for the canal boats to make the voyage from the Hudson River to Buffalo. The boats were flat-bottomed rafts that usually measured eighty feet long by fifteen feet wide. The famous British writer Charles Dickens called the canal boat he rode "a barge with a little house in it." The boats were laboriously tugged by a team of two or three horses or mules that walked the towpath alongside the ditch.

A remarkable new society developed along the canal banks. Soon after its opening, more than four thousand boats plowed back and forth on the waterway. To service the boat tenders and passengers, grocery stores, supply outlets, saloons, and hotels sprang up at canal side. Towns and villages rose, seemingly overnight, in spots where once there had been only barren woods. Buffalo grew from a sleepy village to a booming city in less than a decade.

The success of the Erie Canal touched off a canal-building craze in other areas of the United States. By 1840, more than four thousand miles of canals laced the countryside. The most ambitious of them was the Grand Canal, which cut across the heart of

Pennsylvania and connected Philadelphia with Pittsburgh. But dozens of complications robbed the new canals of the income enjoyed by the Erie Canal. Most of them fell into disuse after the development of the railroad system.

The Erie Canal, however, thrived even into the railroad era. Business was so good that over the years the state had to widen the ditch and modernize the locks several times over. Even today, the Erie Canal is the longest section of what is now the New York State Barge Canal System. Many of the original locks and ditches were destroyed as the canal was re-dug over and over again to permit the passage of larger and more-efficient boats.

But even in the 1980s, a curious visitor to upstate New York can find relics of the old Erie Canal. Sadly, some portions of the great ditch have become dumping grounds for junk cars, mattress springs, and beer cans. Yet the brickwork that lined the waterway's sides still stands unflawed as a tribute to the workmanship of those long-ago masons. A visitor with an active imagination can gaze at a weed-infested portion of the original canal and picture the time when this forgotten ditch served to open the western half of a blossoming American

nation. The visitor might also let his thoughts dance
back a century and more to the days when teamsters
drove their animals over the towpaths, dragged the
barges behind them, and sang this lively song:

> I've got a mule and her name is Sal,
> Fifteen miles on the Erie Canal.
> She's a good old worker and a good old pal,
> Fifteen miles on the Erie Canal.
> We've hauled some barges in our day,
> Filled with lumber, coal, and hay,
> And we know every inch of the way
> From Albany to Buffalo.

About the Author

R. Conrad Stein was born and grew up in Chicago. He enlisted in the Marine Corps at the age of eighteen and served for three years. He then attended the University of Illinois where he received a bachelor's degree in history. He later studied in Mexico, earning an advanced degree from the University of Guanajuato. Mr. Stein is the author of many other books, articles, and short stories written for young people.

Mr. Stein now lives in Chicago with his wife, Deborah Kent, who is also a writer of books for young readers, and their daughter Janna.

About the Artist

Keith Neely attended the School of the Art Institute of Chicago and received a Bachelor of Fine Arts degree with honors from the Art Center College of Design where he majored in illustration. He has worked as an art director, designer, and illustrator and has taught advertising illustration and advertising design at Biola College in La Mirada, California. Mr. Neely is currently a freelance illustrator whose work has appeared in numerous magazines, books, and advertisements. He lives with his wife and five children in Florida.

Children's Pass

Stein, R. Conrad
AUTHOR

The Erie Canal
TITLE

DATE DUE	BORROWER'S NAME	ROOM NUMBER
4/15	Denning	6a